Pure Confi

C000059719

Walk your own path
for the rest of your living days.

Amy Elizabeth

This book is dedicated to my son, and all those who have helped me find my own inner peace, release my ego, and maximise my self-belief.

With you every step of the way...

I empower people to help themselves. I help people bring their lives to a cohesive whole. It is my intention to help as many people in as many ways as I can, and I hope that this book goes some way towards offering help and support to those of you who need it.

Beyond the pages of this book, you will find other sources of support (see page 79 and beyond for further guidance).

"There aren't many people I've met with the same unbridled level of energy and passion as Amy - if you're looking for someone to unlock your potential, understand who you are and what makes your heart sing, Amy can do just that. Through her book, cards and associated projects, she can teach us all a thing or two about the importance of living a joyful life, thinking more deeply and growing fully into your best self."

- Emma Sasai, Editor and Copywriter

About the Author

Amy Elizabeth is a heart-centred entrepreneur on a mission to inspire, energise and empower as many people as she can to live happy and fulfilling lives.

Having risen above adverse circumstances to achieve positive stability and success in her own life, Amy has a strong desire to help and support others, particularly young people.

Amy has learned how to change her beliefs, thoughts and self-talk so that she is no longer living in an 'if only' mindset; she now sees possibility in everything, enabling her to live a more resilient and creative life.

As well as running her own dance school, designing jewellery and clothing lines and mentoring young people, Amy is trained in multiple healing practices including Reiki, The Bars - Access Consciousness, Hopi Ear Candles and Crystal Healing. She is also mother to a young son and passionate about protecting animals and working to save our planet.

"I've learnt to be thankful and I've learnt how to be happy. If you want happiness for a lifetime, help others."

CONTENTS

CONTENTS

INTRODUCTION

Self-confidence, or belief in oneself, is important for virtually everything.

It helps us talk to that person, take that action, and stand our ground in the face of fear or ridicule.

Self-belief ultimately plays a part in almost everything we do, so taking the time to cultivate more of it is incredibly worthwhile.

And to help you do that, I've written this book.

The book covers a lot of ground – from developing belief in yourself and your efforts, as well as realising your goals, developing more positive mental habits, improving your relationships, and practising self-care.

Throughout the book, I use the words 'self-esteem' and 'self-confidence' interchangeably, even if there is a subtle but perhaps important difference … the difference being whether you believe you're worthy of respect from others (self-esteem) and whether you believe in yourself (self-confidence). In the end, both amount to the same thing, and in the end, the insights, techniques and tasks I mention throughout the book are there to give a boost to both self-esteem and self-confidence.

So if you're looking to build confidence and belief in yourself, I hope that you will find something within these pages that will help you do just that.

How this book came to be

Self-confidence is hugely important. It determines what levels of success you achieve and how much joy you have in your life. It can raise or lower the quality of your treasured relationships. I don't feel anyone formally verses us in the art of being confident, and while our parents may have encouraged us to believe that we could do something (if we were lucky enough to have that level of support), I don't feel we grew up realising its significance.

I first became aware of my self-confidence at a young age, probably when I was about 5 or 6 years old. At the same time, I also recognised how this could easily be crushed by another person or a bad experience, and how I had to almost fight to keep hold of my confidence. Obviously it wasn't as clear-cut as I make it sound here. It was all very confusing to be honest. I am very headstrong and have been since childhood, so perhaps this is what underpins my confidence – my sheer determination to hold onto it.

As I grew up, I became more and more self aware, and increasingly attuned to the behaviour of others. I became more aware of the kind of situations that made me feel confident, the people who boosted my confidence, how to make the most of my confidence, and how to inspire confidence in others.

However, I haven't always been brimming with confidence. Far from it. I have had many experiences where my confidence has been shattered – to almost nothing. Few things are more detrimental than low levels of self-confidence. At those times when I wasn't feeling confident in myself, I didn't take risks, I didn't enjoy life and I usually ended up stuck in places I didn't want to be.

However bad things got, I always knew that I needed to build myself back up and reclaim my usual high levels of self-confidence. When you believe in yourself and your abilities, you take smart risks, achieve important goals and develop meaningful relationships with those around you. It's a much happier place.

There have been ups and downs; I am human after all. But I have reached a point now where I have established a happy medium; my confidence works for me. I recognise that I am a work in progress, and I have to work on my confidence daily, which can mean stepping beyond my comfort zone. As long as I remind myself that it all starts in the mind, I can take those challenging steps or give myself that push I need to overcome what it is holding me back so that I can pursue my dreams.

I still have fears. We all do. But I know that we can beat them and break through that wall of fear and come out on the other side. I have done it many times, and that success is what fuels further success.

Self-confidence is the best outfit, claim it, rock it and – most importantly – own it.

Without going into too much more detail about all the highs and lows of my relationship with myself, I will say one thing – so far it has been a wonderful journey of learning. I have learnt to accept and love myself, and now I am ready to learn more and extend what I have learnt to others in any way I can.

Which is where this book comes into play.

I have always loved to help others. Ever since finishing formal education, I have invested a lot of myself in learning how to reach out and offer support and encouragement to others, especially young people.

I have a special understanding with children of all ages and young adults; I can recognise and read their emotions, and I know what to say to them to make them feel better about themselves and inspire them to take action. I think this can be attributed to the times when I have had to be resilient in the face of adversity and learn to manage a number of difficult situations. I have a high level of emotional intelligence – I am able to read other people, I know what they are about, I understand what they are going through – I just 'get' them. I am naturally curious about everyone around me, I care about what they're going through, and I think this is why I seem to develop strong relationships with people.

It also explains my constant thirst for knowledge and learning, particularly at a deep emotional level.

Over the years, I have acquired a number of qualifications, and most of them hold a link to helping other people. I have a degree in Dance, and am a qualified dance teacher and choreographer, I am a freelance drama facilitator, a fashion and jewellery designer – all these titles have enabled me to help many people. I also hold qualifications in Reiki, Crystal Healing, and Hopi ear candles; I am a Bars Facilitator (touching points on the head to release energy); I am also a volunteer with Macmillan Cancer Support and the Teenage Cancer Trust.

My list of skills and experience is long, so I won't go into any more detail here, but I have come to see that all that I have pursued on my journey so far comes from the heart – and my desire to empower others, whether that's through designing a range of clothing which gives the wearer more confidence in how they present themselves, teaching dance skills that help people believe in themselves and their abilities or giving treatments to people to help them unlock energy and open up possibility.

Thanks to all that I have learned, I have figured out some really great ways to grow and retain confidence – in mind, body, and spirit. And I want to share those ways with as many people as I can. Ultimately, it is my desire to guide people towards understanding themselves more so that they can self-heal just as I have done.

I hope that within the pages of this book, you will find some helpful insights and techniques that will enable you to ignite your self-belief, self-esteem, self-love and self-confidence.

Amen.

Confidence – where does it come from?

Do you ever wonder what it is about some people that makes them so confident? So completely comfortable in their skin, radiating such positive, charismatic energy? We all know someone like this. I remember the first time I met my son's art teacher. She was completely at peace with who she was in every moment, interaction and experience. She radiated positive, charismatic energy – and she wasn't a particularly extroverted personality. She was just content with who she was. No apologies. No excuses. Just herself.

I used to wonder where these qualities came from. She appeared to just 'float', glide around with elegance somehow. I can see her now gliding across the school car park with her books and bags. How come she oozed all that confidence? Where did it come from?

Confidence really comes down to one incredibly simple thing. Owning it. My son's teacher fully owned it.

Now it's one thing to recognise that you need to settle into accepting who you are; it's another to be able to connect with and 'own' your feelings, emotions and sensations at any given moment, and not give a single thought to what other people are thinking.

That's where this book comes in – to help you appear and (more importantly) feel confident no matter what.

"I'm 97% sure you don't like me, but I'm 100% sure I don't care."

How to get the most out of the book

I hope this book gives you the energy and motivation to dig a little deeper to look at your own levels of confidence, and how you can work to enhance your self-esteem, self-belief and self-confidence. I hope the book gives you the opportunity to reflect, and identify areas for improvement, i.e., where you feel you may lack confidence and how you can then start to change that.

Throughout the book, you will find short exercises and tasks to help you organise your thoughts and really get your mind working differently, towards making some real positive changes.

As you work your way through the book, I hope that you will make notes, particularly when you do one of the tasks. That is why I have created **The Positivity Journal**.

Journaling is a beautiful and powerful facilitator of self-discovery. My own journaling is how I've come to form my sense of identity and path in life. Not only will you have more clarity about your path in life, but you will find that you are more able to make small and large decisions along the way. The pages of your journal will be the building blocks for the future world you are creating for yourself.

"You are the author of your life's story. You have the power to create whatever life you want. "

The Positivity Journal is an interactive journal with lots of space for you to record and reflect on your emotions, intentions and energy. It is designed to help you think about your current confidence level, set goals to help increase it and be more positive and confident in every area of your life.

Filled with inspiring tips and exercises that will guide you towards mindfully building confidence helping you achieve long-term happiness and a fulfilling life.

I hope you come away from this book with a deeper understanding of yourself, and a raised self-awareness which you can use going forwards on a journey to a more confident you.

Your journal can take on whatever shape or form you want it to. It doesn't have to be a literary masterpiece, nor a well organised series of beautifully articulate thoughts. Maybe you just want to jot down a few bullet points, or draw a mind map. However you choose to use it is entirely up to you. One thing I will emphasise is how important it is to make notes, as they will serve as a useful gauge of your confidence levels, which I hope you will see change each time you return to review your notes. Making big shifts in your life takes time, it's not an overnight process, so have faith in the book and give it the time needed for its magic to take effect!

"It is important to remember that we all have magic inside us."
J.K. Rowling

This book and **The Positivity Journal** are two parts of **The Positivity Pack**. The third element are my **Confidence Cards** (coming soon). This versatile set of cards can be used to boost morale, and guide you further on your journey of self-discovery. **The Positivity Pack** also includes a downloadable app, which gives you access to podcasts, daily boosts, and an array of supportive and motivational material – ideal for when you are on the go (all coming soon - watch this space).

All of these 'add-ons' provide broader and meaningful ways for you to work on your confidence – in any which way you choose to. This can simply be flicking to a particular page in this book, choosing one of the tasks to complete and doing it when you feel a need for a boost. Or you may choose to use the the **Confidence Cards**, listening to a podcast one morning, or using **The Positivity Journal** to explore your own emotions ... the combinations are endless; each and every one of you will have a different experience. I hope that you will take from the help offered what you feel is relevant, what you feel drawn to and what is right for you.

Although this book has a numerical order and can be read from start to finish, it works just as well if you want to dip in and out of it as and when you feel you need to.

One thing that works for me is to flick the pages of the book, stop suddenly and see which page I've landed on – then I read the content of that page, and it is usually just what I need at that point in time. Try it!

What is confidence?

Let's start by doing what many of us do when we need an answer to a question – Google it! Here's what Google has to say:

"Confidence comes from feelings of well-being, acceptance of your body and mind (self-esteem) and belief in your own abilities, skills and experience."

That sums it up very well. For me, having confidence starts with taking action. We all want to do or try certain things but fear they are beyond our reach and we worry about failing. Those nerves are normal – everyone has them. The difference between a person who is confident and a person who is not is simply that the confident person acts on their ambitions and desires, and doesn't let that fear of failure stop them.

"Confidence is life's enabler – it is the quality that turns thoughts into action."

Psychology Dictionary Online defines self-confidence as "an individual's trust in his or her own abilities, capacities, and judgements, or belief that he or she can successfully face day to day challenges and demands."

This definition also really resonates with me, particularly in my role as a parent. I am a single mum to a 7-year-old son, and I am constantly trying to strike that very delicate balance of giving him the support and protection he needs along with enough independence to nurture competence and confidence. There's an old saying about giving your children roots and wings. I love this. My unconditional love is the roots and confidence is the wings. If I can supply these two things, I know he will be set up to live a big and happy life.

What makes a confident person?

I'm sure we all know people who have confidence written all over them, and they seem largely unaware of it, too; they just 'are'. Then there are the confident kids at school who seem to handle every situation thrown at them with ease, and it's possible that you thought they were very different to you in that respect – however, the only difference lies in their attitude.

A confident person knows that, if they are doing something for the first time, it's a new experience and mistakes are inevitable, and whatever happens will be all right.

I've met a lot of confident people; in fact, I am very attracted to them. I enjoy and share their positive outlook on life. In my experience, these are a few of the attributes that make a person confident:

Confident people…

· Have faith in their own abilities

· Are comfortable with uncertainty

· Know they can handle failure if it happens

· Believe they can cope; not necessarily succeed – there's a difference!

· Don't feel they have to conform in order to be accepted

· Are willing to risk the disapproval of others because they trust their own judgement

· Don't need the approval of others, hence their ability to tolerate failure

· Can see the funny side of things, even personal mistakes and misfortunes

· Don't take things too seriously or personally

· Feel good about themselves

· Make others feel good about themselves

TASK -
'About Me' - start thinking about your own levels of confidence

This is an activity that both adults and children can engage in. You can work through the sentences alone or with your child/ children, or anyone else you feel may benefit from the task.

The 'About Me' task is intended to help you identify your own positive traits and characteristics, and recognise your accomplishments.

It's a simple list with six sentence prompts and space for you (or your child) to fill in. You can write your answers in **The Positivity Journal** or a notebook, or you could use sticky notes and put them in places where you can see them often, as you go about your day.

The six sentence prompts are:

I am really happy when...

Something that my friends like about me is...

I'm proud of...

My family is happy when I…

In my educational surroundings / my career, I am good at…

Something that makes me unique is…

Take your time to think about each sentence, and encourage your child/children to do so too if they are doing the task.

This activity will get you really thinking about yourself in a positive frame of mind; for children, it can help build the foundations of an authentic and healthy self-esteem that they can carry with them for the rest of their life.

3

Confidence in the Early Years

My young son is confident because I have allowed him to be, and have strived to fill him with confidence whenever he has doubted himself.

Friends comment on how confident he is in all he does. I know this is because I won't have it any other way.

Whenever I see my son doubting himself, I help him to turn the situation around immediately. Over time, he has come to see that confidence is a choice.

He also models his behaviour on those around him, particularly mine.

I am always mindful of my actions and words around him as I know how influential they can be on his development. Even if I am not feeling so good about myself, I try to turn this around. After all, it's my job as a parent to encourage and support him, particularly when he has to tackle difficult tasks.

As parents, we need to strike a balance, and allow them to walk their own path, giving useful feedback and suggestions as they do so, without doing all the work for them. It's hard at times not to be over-protective of our children, but they need to mess things up in order to learn how to do a better job next time.

Treat mistakes as an opportunity to learn and grow. Engage them in thinking that we 'fail forwards' and that there is no such thing as failure; we either win or we learn.

Exposing children to new experiences teaches them that no matter how scary and different something may at first appear, they can conquer it.

Until the teen years, you are your child's hero, so use that power to teach them what you know about how to think, act, and speak. Set a good example, and be a role model. Watching you succeed will help your child be more confident that they can do the same.

I often take my son to dance rehearsals with me when he is off school. He sees me take a lead role. He sees my confidence shining. He particularly enjoys and appreciates when I work with performers with disabilities as they develop differently. He joins in and stands at the front with me to help them. He likes to show them his dance skills also. This is so beautiful to witness.

I often make him part of my journey. Recently he came to watch as I completely stepped out of my comfort zone as I stood in front of investors to pitch for money. He knows this is not an everyday encounter for me, and he gets to see me pump my confidence into something that is quite scary for me.

He also recently witnessed me 'fail' an exam. He said, "What will you do now, Mum? Are you upset?" I let him know that I simply wasn't ready for the exam so I will try again and pass, and I will think very carefully in the future about putting so much pressure on myself like I did in this situation. He applauds me for my resilience and my 'get up and try again' attitude. I hope he will absorb this into his own life in the future.

One of my practices is to write myself affirmations on sticky notes and stick them around the house. When I catch sight of one of my notes, I say it out loud. Without any prompting from me, my son sticks his own notes on his bedroom wall. And just as I do, he reads them out loud, over and over.

I always applaud his successes, I give constructive criticism, I use positive affirmations with him daily, I share decision making with him, I give him choices and of course I act confidently in front of him.

Children with high levels of self-confidence perform better at school and, later in life, have higher levels of job satisfaction. Self-esteem is also strongly linked to happiness, with higher levels of self-esteem predicting higher levels of happiness. High self-confidence has even been found to increase chances of survival after a serious surgical procedure (Mann et al., 2004)!

There's no doubt about it. Confidence is one of the greatest gifts a parent can give a child.

TASK - Make and use positive affirmations

Affirmations are a popular way to help combat low self-esteem in both adults and adolescents. Certainly one of my favourite ways to build confidence is through positive affirmations. In short, these are positive and uplifting statements that we say to ourselves. They are normally more effective if said out loud so that you can hear yourself say it. We believe whatever we tell ourselves constantly. For example, if you hate your own physical appearance, practise saying something that you appreciate or like about yourself when you next look in the mirror.

To get your brain to accept your positive statements more quickly, phrase your affirmations as questions like, "Why am I so good at helping other people?" instead of "I am so good at helping other people." Our brains are biologically wired to seek answers to questions, without analysing whether the question is valid or not.

I use mirror pens and write quotes on my mirrors each week, and as I mentioned earlier in the book, I write on sticky notes and stick them in places where I will read them the most (usually somewhere near the kettle!). I also write positive affirmations throughout my diary so that I keep reading them each week. I own lots of items that have positive quotes on them (my house is filled with positive wall art, tea cups, placemats, notebooks, pens – pretty much anything I can lay my hands on!)

Here are some guidelines for producing effective affirmations:

- Affirmations start with the words "I am…"
- Affirmations are positive. Never use the word 'not' in an affirmation.
  For example, instead of writing "I am not afraid of public speaking" you could write "I am a confident speaker."
- Affirmations are short and specific.
  For example, instead of writing "I am driving a new car" you could write "I am driving a new black Range Rover."
- Affirmations are in the present tense.
- Affirmations have a 'feeling' word in them.
  Examples include "confidently," "successfully," or "gracefully."
- Affirmations are about yourself.
- Affirmations should be about your own behaviour, never someone else's.

Use **The Positivity Journal** or a notebook to write down some affirmations of your own. It's okay to refer back to the guidelines as much as you need.

Now that you have your affirmations, what next? What do you do with them?

· Say and visualise your affirmations every day, ideally when you wake up, at lunch time and before you go to bed. Watch them come to life in your mind.

· Take time to see yourself accomplishing the goals you've set.

· Think about how good it will feel once you have accomplished your goals – feel that feeling you would feel when the goal is accomplished.

· Write new affirmations as and when. Your life constantly changes, and so should your affirmations.

Affirmations are life-changing. When you use them over and over, you will be working towards rewiring your mind. Remember that writing down and then saying affirmations is only part of the process. What you do the rest of the day and night is even more important. The secret to having your affirmations work is to prepare an atmosphere for them to grow in. Each time you say an affirmation, it's like you are planting a seed in soil. If the soil is poor, there will be no growth. Rich soil, on the other hand will bring abundant growth. So create the surroundings for your affirmations to thrive. This means thinking thoughts that make you feel good. It's that simple. The more you do this, the quicker the affirmations work. Live and breathe your affirmations. Visualise them, believe in them and achieve them. It is important to know that only YOU can make them your reality. You make them grow!

4

My 7 Lessons for Practising Self-Confidence

I would like to share my 'go-to' ways of giving myself a boost when I need it. They are short and sweet, and can be done anywhere. Try one per day for a week and notice how you feel at the end of the week. If you want to, you can note down your feelings in **The Positivity Journal** and keep going for a month, and then read over your notes, and see how your feelings and levels of confidence have changed. Even small differences are significant.

LESSON 1 Stand or Sit in a Posture of Confidence
I love this lesson because it makes me feel empowered.

An individual's posture does not just reflect levels of confidence or insecurity. It also sends messages to the brain that informs you exactly how you feel. That being said, if you need to feel confident, you want your posture to send your brain that message.

Stretch your limbs as far as they will go and make your body as big as you can as soon as you wake up.

Throughout the day, make sure you stand tall, sit up straight, and have a smile on your face. It makes a big difference!

LESSON 2 Practise Presence
I love this lesson because it makes me feel connected.

Similar to the concept of mindfulness, proven to be very beneficial for your physical and psychological well-being. You can practice mindfulness anytime, anywhere. You can give it a try right now by following these steps:

- Become aware of your awareness; that is, begin to observe yourself and your surroundings

- Start with your body sensations, feeling your feet and legs, your stomach and chest, your arms, neck and head.

- Now notice your breath, flowing in and out, and the many sensations that you are experiencing

- Let your eyes notice what is in your visual field, your ears, what they are hearing. Perhaps sensations of smell and taste will come to your awareness as well.

- Then, go beyond these simple sensations to feel the energy, the quiet, or the noises that surround you. Feel your presence.

LESSON 3 Build Your Capacity for Energy
I love this lesson because it makes me perform better. It also makes me feel like an excited child again, as it helps release nerves, replacing them with excitement.

I love speaking to an audience, but I also get a little nervous as each experience is different. So I keep focused on the excitement of the event. In turn, this brings me boosted energy that is needed for any kind of public speaking I do.

Nerves can be useful to keep us on our toes and give us the extra energy needed to perform. Try to re-frame your nervous jitters as excitement! Knowing how to engage with these feelings in your body will expand your presence rather than shrinking it down.

LESSON 4 Exercise Regularly

I love this lesson because it sets me up for the day – in both body and mind.

I make sure I attend a hot yoga class at least once a week as the difference this practice brings to my life is immense. My mind is so calm for the day ahead. On other days I walk my dog each morning. This allows me to expand my thoughts and get focused for the day ahead. This has a positive effect on all I do, gives me more patience as a parent, more focus in my work, and more productivity in my day overall.

Exercise has a powerful effect on so many areas of our life, including our levels of confidence. Regular exercise releases endorphins, which in turn interact with receptors in the brain. This brings a type of pleasurable state of mind, which means you'll view yourself in a more positive light. When you are regularly doing this, not only will you get better physically but you will also feel more motivated to act in ways that build your self-confidence.

LESSON 5 Imagine Confidence

I love this lesson because it is super powerful. Beyond powerful.

Visualisation has changed my life. Period. How can we achieve something if we can't first see it? I saw myself speaking in front of audiences well before I actually got up and gave my first talk. Once I achieved that, I started visualising bigger audiences and now I visualise myself doing TED talks (which, at the time of writing, I have not yet done).

Visualisation brings what you want into your life. For example, if you want to be free of the drama in your life, then you visualise a peaceful life where drama doesn't feature.

TASK

Try this simple exercise: Close your eyes and relax your body completely.

Stay firmly connected with the sensation of relaxation and, in your mind's eye, see yourself speaking on camera or doing whatever activity it is that requires you to step out of your comfort zone, or have more confidence.

Allow the feelings of comfortable presence pervade your body and your mind. The more you practise this, the more familiar the feelings will become, and you will be able to tackle the tasks that previously induced feelings of stress or fear with more presence, and in turn greater confidence.

LESSON 6 Give Yourself Permission to be in the Process, Take Risks and Make Mistakes

I love this lesson because taking risks and making mistakes have got me to this stage of my journey.

This book would not be what it is without the learning I have experienced along the way. Confident people take risks and make mistakes. They learn and move forward with more confidence.

From the outside, it's easy to look at other people and think, "Wow, everybody else is happier, more beautiful, creative, successful, active, etc. than me. I'm just not as good as them". What we are not considering is that failure is inherent in accomplishment and that in order to pursue our goals, we have to work hard and face our weaknesses. Even those who appear super successful or exceptional in some areas of life are likely struggling in others.

Allow yourself to be a learner, to be a novice. It's OK to not be perfect! In fact, you'll likely provide inspiration to others in similar situations.

When breaking out of your comfort zone and starting something new, you are expanding your own limitations, and when you successfully complete something that is out of your confidence zone, you are building confidence in yourself.

LESSON 7 Speak Well to Yourself

I love this lesson because if you can't speak well to yourself, you cannot speak well to others.

It's always delightful to get good feedback from others. However, always seeking approval from outside yourself is an easy trap.

Approve of yourself; be the one that says the words of encouragement you long to hear.

Speak to yourself with kindness, compassion and encouragement. After all, the most important relationship you have in your life is with yourself, so make it a good one!

"Your relationship with yourself sets the tone for every other relationship in your life."

SUMMARY

Remember, as you incorporate these exercises into your daily life, it's a process. Changes will be incremental. Don't expect an overnight transformation! The bottom line is that a healthy sense of self-confidence is not something that we achieve once and then just have for the rest of our lives. If you are a parent, teacher, or someone else who interacts with children frequently, stop trying to build the child's self-esteem through protecting and praising them without warrant. Consider what you are encouraging the child to learn from their actions, provide them with enough opportunities to safely learn through failure, and offer them space to build their courage and express their self-efficacy.

No matter how confident they are, sooner than you think, there will be a moment when they will need to draw from a deep well of self-esteem, resilience, and problem-solving to successfully navigate a complex and challenging world.

And it doesn't stop at childhood. Self-confidence comes and goes, and takes a lifetime of work to build, develop and maintain. We all experience moments which challenge our confidence, however, when we understand the sources of healthy self-confidence, we can always work on cultivating it within ourselves.

TASK
Take a look at the following questions and consider how you would answer them. You can write down your answers in **The Positivity Journal** or a notebook.

What do you think about the challenge of building self-confidence?

Which of the exercises have you tried?

Which ones have had a positive impact on your confidence?

Maybe you've found some other ways to assist in practising self-confidence?

What are they?

5

Confidence – an ongoing process

People tell me that I have a lot of self-confidence. I wasn't
born with it though. No one is. Confidence is something that
we have to work on, some of us more than others. It is a
lifelong pursuit. If you have started to try some of the
exercises in this book, then that's fantastic. You have taken
some really important steps towards building and instilling a
greater sense of confidence in yourself. You now need to keep
building it – for life! It's something that needs constant
attention because we live in a world where we can be
presented with any number of challenging situations at any
given time, and these situations, in general, tend to deflate our
confidence. I speak from experience. Whenever I have taken a
knock, either professionally or personally, my confidence has
been dented as well. So I need to build it back up again.

We've all been there – a well-meaning but sometimes unkind
comment from a loved one, that inner critic rearing its head
telling us we're not good enough, a rejection from a business
associate, a negative review for your products or services …
there are so many elements that threaten our self-confidence.
We need to take charge of building it up for ourselves.

TASK - Supercharge your affirmations

I have already mentioned how beneficial I find the practice of using positive affirmations. Follow these steps and your affirmations will be even more effective and powerful.

Step 1: Make a list of what you've always thought of as your negative qualities / things that hold you back. Include any criticisms others have made of you that you've been holding onto — whether it's something your siblings, parents or peers used to say about you when you were a child, or what your boss told you in your last annual review. Don't judge if they're accurate, and remember we all have flaws. This is one of the beauties of being human. Simply make a note of them and look for a common theme, such as "I'm unworthy." This will be a great place to start making a shift in your life. When you write out the recurring belief, notice if you are holding onto it anywhere in your body? For example, do you feel tightness or dread in your heart or stomach? Ask yourself if this unwholesome concept is helpful or productive in your life — and if not, what would be?

Step 2: Now write out an affirmation on the positive aspect of your self-judgement. You may want to use a thesaurus to find more powerful words to beef up your statement! For example, instead of saying, "I'm worthy," you could say, "I'm remarkable and cherished." After you have written your affirmation, ask a close friend to read it to see if they have any suggestions for how to make it stronger. (You don't have to share the experience with a friend – sometimes this process is very personal, and that's absolutely fine; it will still work!) Always work in the most direct positive way with 'I am'.

Step 3: Speak the affirmation out loud for about five minutes three times a day — morning, midday, and evening. The more you can do it, the better!

An ideal time to do this is when you're putting on your make-up or shaving, so that you can look at yourself in the mirror as you repeat the positive statement. Another option that helps to reinforce the new belief is to write out the affirmation several times in **The Positivity Journal** or notebook. Notice over time as you write it if your style of writing changes. This could be a clue as to how your mind perceives the new concept.

Step 4: Anchor the affirmation in your body as you are repeating it by placing your hand on the area that felt uncomfortable when you wrote out the negative belief in Step 1. Also, 'breathe' into the affirmation while you are saying or writing it. As you reprogramme your mind, you want to move from the concept of the affirmation to a real, positive embodiment of the quality you seek. This is a very powerful part of the process – which is why you need to ensure you have carved out time to do it, and your mind doesn't suddenly switch to wondering what time it is, and whether you're going to be late for an appointment / picking up the kids from school.

Step 5: Get a friend or mentor figure to repeat your affirmation to you. (I do this with my son as it then helps me and him in one shot!) If you don't have someone whom you feel comfortable asking, then use your reflection in the mirror as the person who is reinforcing the healthy message.

Affirmations are a powerful tool to help you change your mood, state of mind, and manifest the change you desire in your life. But they work best if you can first identify the unwholesome belief that is opposing them. I don't know how I would live without them!

There are lots of wonderful YouTube videos filled with affirmations for abundance, success, self-esteem and so much more. My recommendations can be found at the end of the book.

TASK - Make your own affirmation jar

If you are feeling creative, try this activity. You can even get your children to help you with making it, or get them to make their own.

You will need an empty jar / box, small pieces of paper to roll up, a pen and a positive mind!

On each of the small pieces of paper, write an affirmation. Try and think of what you believe you are not to help you create the positive affirmation. For example, if you feel you lack confidence, write "I am confident"; if you feel you make poor food choices, write "I am healthy" or "I eat healthy foods". Always write your affirmation in the positive and try and keep them brief. Make as many as you like (or that fit in your jar / box). Roll them up and slot them in the jar / box. Each day, you can draw out an affirmation (or more than one a day if you like).

Carry this with you or stick it somewhere you will read it often. If you feel a need for a pick-me-up, just go read it. Try and also say it out loud. Telling yourself something out loud has a much deeper impact. Tell yourself as much as possible. I often say it three times (just to make sure its gone in!)

Here are some of my favourite affirmations. You can use them as inspiration for the ones you create for your jar or box, or copy them – I won't mind!

I am destined to be prosperous
I am open to receive an abundance of health, wealth and happiness
I am safe
I am confident
I live a joyful life
I am surrounded by abundance
My life is full of abundance
I always have what I need when I need it

I have time
I am happy
I choose to be happy
I am here to make a bigger impact
I make my own choices
My life is mine to create
I am energy
Money flows to me
I attract positive people into my life
I am grateful for every single moment in my life
Magic surrounds me today
I am successful
I know my value and my worth
I am a money magnet
I am wise
I am open to receive
I am worthy
I passionately live a life of abundance and success
I am blessed
I always attract new opportunities and success
I am gifted and talented
I surrender any fears
I deserve health and wealth in abundance
I am surrounded by good honest people
I love myself unconditionally
I feel good about the money that I spend
I share my gifts with others

Of course, your affirmations will be personal to you, and the ones you choose to create do not have to mirror any that have been written or spoken by others, but you may find some overlap, which is why I think it's worth sharing some of the affirmations that I have found particularly effective in building my confidence.

1. I am fearless.

2. I am always improving, but for today, I have the knowledge I need.

3. I am calm and mindful.

4. I am compassionate with others and myself.

5. I am a positive being, aware of my potential.

6. There are no blocks I cannot overcome.

7. I am strong and wise.

8. I love to meet other people and make new friends.

9. Life is beautiful.

10. I am my best source of motivation.

11. Challenges are opportunities to grow and improve.

12. I only attract positive people because I am a positive person myself.

13. I am unique.

14. I make a difference by showing up every day and doing my best.

15. I am becoming a better version of myself one day at a time.

16. My actions are intentional and they bring me closer to my goals.

17. I deserve what I want because my wish is pure and I have the required qualities.

18. I am solution-driven. I am not afraid of obstacles.

19. I am capable of accomplishing my tasks and responsibilities.

20. I am grateful for my journey and its lessons.

21. I have unlimited power.

22. I love myself and the circumstances life presents me.

23. I accept compliments easily because I know I deserve them.

24. Everything and anything is possible.

25. I am creative and open to new solutions.

26. I am talented and intelligent.

27. My work fulfills me.

28. I acknowledge my 'super powers' and use them to assist others.

29. I am enthusiastic, confident and persistent.

30. I let go of fearing mistakes and failure.

Building Confidence

There are so many ways to build confidence. I have touched upon a few already.

It can be as simple as making very small changes, whether it's the way you brush and wear your hair to something bigger such as changing your circle of friends, your job, or your circumstances. These are the ways, both big and small, that will help you become confident in all that you do:

Reframing
We often hear the phrase 'reframing' or 'reframing your mind'. What does it mean exactly and how does it work? Simple. You point your mind in a new direction. You rewire the mind. You remove negativity and replace it with positivity so you are no longer consumed by negative thoughts and/or held back. You lift self-limiting beliefs.

All of this starts with first 'catching your mind out'. Catching it in the act. Basically recognising its behaviour. For example, the ability to catch yourself talking yourself down and then stopping and shifting this. Flipping it on its head and doing the total opposite. All it's really about is recognising your thoughts and your words / actions and analysing them so that you recognise negative behaviour and you quickly flip it. Acting quickly is key here. We can so easily play out a whole negative scenario in our heads which is so far fetched and so far from the truth. The ability to quickly stop this in its tracks is key. STOP! Shake it off and turn your thoughts to something else. Don't dwell on it, we have all been there. In time, you will become a negativity diminishing, thought flipping pro!

How can you shake off negativity? How can you flip a negative into a positive? Here are my top tips on doing just this.

Be mindful of who you are around – are the people around you lifting you higher? Are they encouraging you? Are they filling you with confidence? A great way to test this if you are unsure is to clock how you feel after seeing certain people. Do you feel drained and low in energy? (If so, you may be spending time with 'energy vampires') Do you feel vibrant and excited? They say you equal the sum of the five people you spend most of your time with. Choose wisely. Surround yourself with people who support and lift you higher as well as make you feel happy and light.

Have hot Himalayan salt baths – this is a truly therapeutic and rejuvenating experience for your body, mind and soul. Himalayan pink salt is said to be the purest form of natural salt on Earth today. It contains 84 nourishing trace elements and minerals that cannot be found in regular processed table salt. Having regular Himalayan salt baths can easily boost your immunity, regulate your pH balance, fight off infections such as viral and bacterial assaults on the skin and body, and give your overall wellbeing a terrific boost. It's like soaking in an ocean of energy. As your body organs resonate with the natural frequency of the minerals in the salt bath, your body is being recharged; hence, boosting metabolism and triggering its self-healing powers. This, in turn, works wonders on how you feel about yourself; try it – it's a practical and virtually free step to long-term wellness.

Burn sage – the practice of burning sage, also known as smudging, is an ancient spiritual ritual. For healers in traditional cultures, smudging is used to achieve a healing state, or to solve or reflect upon dilemmas. It can also be used as a ritual tool to rid yourself of negativity, including past traumas, bad experiences or negative energies from others. Ridding the body of bad energy can help welcome in newer, fresher, and more positive energies.

The practice of burning sage or smudging is fairly simple.

You will need:
- a sage bundle (or smudge stick)
- a bowl (ceramic, clay or glass) to hold burning sage or capture ash
- matches
- optional feather or fan for fanning smoke

Before burning sage, you might want to set some intentions if smudging for spiritual, energetic, and negativity-clearing purposes.

It's also important to leave a window open before, during, and after smudging. This allows smoke to escape, along with the impurities and negative energies you want to get rid of.

General practice:

Light the end of a sage bundle with a match. Blow out quickly if it catches on fire.

The tips of the leaves should smoulder slowly, releasing thick smoke. Direct this smoke around your body and space with one hand while holding the bundle in the other.

Allow the incense to linger on the areas of your body or surroundings you'd like to focus on. Using a fan or feather can also help direct the smoke.

Allow the ash to collect in a bowl.

Choose the places you want to smudge, whether that's areas in your home, particular objects, or parts of your body. Do what feels best for your situation and follow your intuition.

Whenever I practise smudging in my home, it feels 'light and right'. I often burn sage when others have been into my home. Some people are unaware of what they are carrying. This then comes into your space. Keep your aura cleansed and your space pure. When I smudge myself, it leaves me feeling incredibly grounded and cleansed in body and mind. I find it a great way to release a lot of negative chatter in my head and bring me back to a more positive place.

Live in the question – This practice opens up lots of possibility and, in many cases, room for improvement. Every day, I try to ask myself a question so that I feel empowered. You don't need to know the answer, you just need to ask. Sometimes I might add a question on the end of an email to someone. For example, 'How can it get any better than this?' No one ever replies with an answer to the question but it doesn't matter. I don't need an answer. It is just opening up possibility – room for 'more'. You don't need to find the answers. Just keep the questions open. And allow answers to come in, whatever form they may take.

Listen to affirmations to uplift you – one of my little tricks is as soon as a negative thought enters my head, I switch to YouTube (if I can) and listen to positive affirmations. When your mind is turned to positive talk, you simply have no room at that time for negative talk.

First see, and then pull out the silver lining – often when we are in a tough situation or are experiencing something 'heavy', we find it very hard to pull out the good because we may not see any. Wrong. There is always a silver lining. Oftentimes we see this much further down the line, but we can also see this at the present time. I find asking myself these questions helps:

- What is / are the lesson(s) here?
- How can it get any better than this?
- What else is possible?
- What do I need to look at?
- Is this trying to nudge me along to something much bigger and better?
- What could I change here?
- What is this showing me?
- What am I learning?

Know you will look back and be grateful for the situation – everything happens for a reason. Period.

Be grateful of the good and the not so good – the not so good situations I have dealt with have strengthened me. I have learned so much from my not so great choices / mistakes and not so good situations. Now when I am dealing with a not so great situation I just learn to be there, and then be grateful for it because I know I will look back on it and be grateful for the changes it may bring. What would life be without challenges, failures, mistakes and off-key emotions? I feel it's where we learn the most and of course grow the most too! Do not apologise for this. Embrace it.

Shut out negative thoughts immediately – here I use a great technique my spiritual leader taught me. I actually sing it in the form of a song. I quite literally 'la, la, la' my thoughts. When a negative thought comes in, I say 'la, la, la' out loud (if possible) over and over until it goes.

Cut your emotional cords via visualisation techniques – I learned this with my spiritual leader, and found it a powerful and helpful way of letting go of things / relationships that no longer served me, enabling me to transition to the next phase of my life.

TASK - Cut Your Cords
Emotional cords are formed on a subconscious level, and severing them is a useful way to clear past experiences, get rid of resentments, and stop repeating old patterns. Cutting the cord does not necessarily sever a relationship, unless that is the intent, rather it puts the relationship back onto a healthy path. It's important, prior to cutting the cords, that you understand how they got formed in the first place and what you can learn from any positive aspects from the relationship.

When you're ready to cut your emotional cords, the method will go something like this…

Relaxation: Get into a comfortable position, either sitting or lying down. Close your eyes to block out external distractions, and take several deep breaths to calm your body down.

Visualise the cords: The next stage involves clearly visualising the person/ thing with which you wish to sever the cords. Take your time to really see and feel the cords that exist between the two of you. Some people visualise them as ropes or chains, while others may see them as electrical cords or rays of light. There is no right or wrong way to visualise the cords. Find what suits you best.

Visualise cutting the cords: Picture yourself physically cutting these negative cords. Some people envisage themselves snipping them with scissors or a sword, while others see themselves unplugging the cords and freeing themselves. Some cords may be a bit tougher to sever than others so give yourself time, and remember to let love in and heal as well.

Awareness and healing: Once the exercise is complete and you're happy that all the emotional cords have been properly severed, it's important to take some time to relax and heal yourself. Imagine a healing energy around the areas where the cords were cut; this is a particularly important step if you were cutting away from a difficult or painful situation.

Future awareness: If you have interactions with that person in the future it's vital that you keep in mind the cord cutting process that you've been through. Aim to establish healthy, positive patterns of interaction with that person from now on to avoid falling back into the negative patterns that you have just severed.

You can do this task as little or as often as you like. Do it until you feel different. Feel the release. Feel the new. (You might want to write down how you feel in **The Positivity Journal**).

Make new choices - If you are feeling dull and low, choose to feel light and energised. You can very easily choose how you feel.

Make healthy food choices - Eat foods and consume drinks that make you feel good.

Keep your mind busy - This is an important one if you are an over-thinker. When you keep your mind busy and focused, you have no time for an over-thinking session in that head of yours.

Get busy living - Stop worrying, start living! We hear it all the time. Live the best life you can. Live the life you have dreamed for yourself. Create the life you would like.

Stay true to you - You know who you are. Continue to be you. If that means getting a whole new set of friends who are the same page as you, then go ahead and do so. Go find your tribe.

Keep it fresh - We are constantly evolving (some more so than others and obviously at different paces / frequencies, and all in different directions to one another) and we need to keep it fresh. How boring would it be to go through life being the same as you have always been? You can be consistent without being the same all the time. For example, I have been consistent in following my core values, but I have practised many different ways of living. When I was younger I wanted a vibrant city life, and now I love the peace and tranquility of the countryside.

Change – I love change, I welcome it. It's good for you. It's the only constant in life. Change inspires change, and change is not always scary. Without it, we would likely remain in the same place for our entire life and where's the excitement in that? We're constantly progressing and transforming every single day and it's important that we learn to embody change with open arms rather than reprehend it. Change allows us to move forward and help us heal our wounds. When you start focusing on new circumstances and new reasons to be happy, you'll stop paying attention to what no longer deserves a place in your life. Each and every change reveals something new about yourself that you didn't pay attention to before.

"Change is always good!"

Meditate – Meditation builds confidence through letting everything go. If you think about it, feeling confident is almost always accompanied by a complete lack of thinking. You're in the zone … you don't think, you just do!

By meditating regularly, it becomes easier to 'get in the zone', turn your brain off, and stop negative self-talk. Studies have found that meditation increases social self-confidence, sociability, general psychological health, and social maturity.

It also offers a wealth of other benefits, including:

Reducing stress
Helping control anxiety
Enhancing self-awareness
Generating kindness
Helping with addictions
Promoting emotional wellbeing
Helping focus and attention span
Aiding memory (and also age-related issues such as memory loss)
Increasing positive feelings
Helping to nurture forgiveness
Improving sleep
Helping control pain

Meditation is not something that you can do just once or twice and instantly reap all of the benefits. The same way you need to brush your teeth every day to keep them clean and healthy, you need to meditate consistently to keep your mind quiet and confident. Try to make meditation part of your day, even if it's 5-10 minutes first thing in the morning, or last thing at night. I think that you'll see a noticeable difference (in terms of your ability to stay out of your head and feel more confident) after about two weeks … but don't expect to meditate today and wake up with superhero-level confidence tomorrow morning!

Here's a simple meditation to get you started:
Before you begin, find a quiet place where you won't be disturbed.

Set a timer for the length of time you want to meditate. If you are a complete beginner, I recommend starting with just two minutes, then increasing the time as you become more comfortable and your ability to focus grows. Just choose what seems doable to you on that particular day.

Then find a comfortable position to sit – it can be in a chair, crossed-legged, on your knees, or lying down.

Place your hands on your belly, relax your body, and listen to your breath. Don't do anything to try to control your breath – simply observe.

Now, bring in some visualisation. As you exhale, picture an ocean wave breaking on the sand. As you inhale, see it rolling back into the sea. With every inhale and exhale, watch the waves go in and out – the sound of your breath is the soundtrack to these waves going in and out, and will set the pace.

If your mind wanders, bring yourself back to the sound of your breathing and the images of the waves. Do not try to change your breathing in any way – simply match the motion of the waves to the sound of your breath.

You may find that the shapes of the waves change throughout your meditation session. I often begin with more powerful waves crashing on the beach (breathing harder) and end with waves that are barely lapping the shore, as my breathing calms and I become more relaxed. This is not a goal, just something to observe.

Feel free to experiment with what works for your visualisations, making the exercise your own. When your timer goes off, take your time, and don't stand up too quickly. Observe how you feel; notice the changes. Embrace the calm.

There are so many choices when it comes to developing a meditation practice. So enjoy exploring – you'll soon see there's a meditation for almost anything! Just check out the huge array of choice on YouTube.

You can find my personal recommendations at the end of the book, but remember that what works for me won't necessarily work for you, and you will probably have to try several methods to find the one that suits you best.

When it comes to the effects on your levels of confidence, meditation essentially trains your brain to dissociate itself from the constant 'mental chatter' going on inside your head – the 'mental chatter' that causes you to lose confidence and get anxious in the first place. Meditation allows you to realise that you don't have to listen to the voice inside your head … especially when it's being negative and focusing on 'bad' things about yourself (e.g. how you look, what people think about you, etc). Think of it this way: when you're feeling confident it's almost always accompanied by a complete lack of thinking. You're in the zone… you don't think, you just do! So developing a meditation practice will work wonders for your confidence … enough said!

"Happiness comes from you. No one else can make you happy. You make you happy."

6

Confidence and Body Language

Slight modifications to your body posture can have a huge impact on not only the impression that you give, but the way you feel about yourself as well.

We stand and walk a certain way when we're confident and another way when we're nervous. In a glance, most people can discern if we're apprehensive or outgoing, relaxed or aggressive. With a little practice, we can learn ways to show confidence through body language so that we always appear confident, capable and ready.

Here are a few tips to increase your confidence through practising confident body language.

Stand Straight – Don't slouch! Those with social anxiety tend to try and take up as little space as possible, which can mean sitting slumped over in a protective pose. Straighten your back, pull your shoulders away from your ears, and uncross your arms and legs.

Chin Up – Where do you look when you are walking? Is it towards the ground? Is your head always down? Instead, try walking with your head up and your eyes looking forward. It might feel unnatural at first, but eventually you will become used to this more confident pose.

Make eye contact – When engaging with another person, face them directly, look them in the eye. Confident people look at others. They do not need to scan their environment in search of threats. They hold people with their gaze, which is relaxed – no narrowing or opening wide the eyes!

Stop fidgeting – Whether it's jingling coins in your pocket, tapping your foot repeatedly on the ground or twirling your hair, stop fidgeting as it betrays a lack of confidence. These movements can also take away from the message you're trying to communicate and may distract people from getting to know you. Pay attention to what triggers your fidgeting habits, and attempt to replace those habits when you experience those triggers.

Dress with confidence – I am not talking about wearing the latest fashion trend – it's all about feeling good in what you're wearing, looking poised and feeling self-assured in all situations. How you dress is related in some way to how you feel. People tend to feel first and dress later. Think of a time when you didn't feel well – did you want to pull out all the stops and dress smart? Not likely. You probably pulled on whatever was closest to you and dressed the way you felt – not that well.

"If we change the way we dress, the way we feel will change."

When we are dressed well and look good, we automatically feel better. When we feel good we are more likely to feel good inside, have more energy and treat others better.

Wear bright colours to lift your mood and put a spring in your step - Colour is the magic that brings interest to our world. We are instinctively drawn to certain colours and respond to them with feeling. The right colours will make your eyes sparkle and your skin glow; while the wrong colours will make you look tired and your skin drab. This is why it is important to know the colours that look best on you. Sit in front of a mirror, place different colours next to your face and notice which colours make your skin come alive and which ones wash it out. When you discover which colours look best on you and wear them consistently, you will notice that you look better, feel better and have more confidence. Pay attention to the comments people make about the colours you wear. If they say a colour suits you, they are essentially saying that it lifts you – and projects who you are.

Step out of your comfort zone (from time to time) – The comfort zone is a useful psychological concept that can help you embrace risk and make changes in your life that can lead to real personal growth. In our comfort zone, there is a sense of familiarity, security and certainty. When we step outside of our comfort zone, we're taking a risk, and opening ourselves up to the possibility of stress and anxiety; we're not quite sure what will happen and how we'll react. We're wired to seek out comfort, which is why it's so hard to let it go. There's nothing wrong with being in your comfort zone, unless you get too comfortable and start holding yourself back instead of challenging yourself to learn, grow and try new things.

Being slightly uncomfortable, whether or not by choice, can push us to achieve goals we never thought we could. But it's important to remember that we don't need to challenge ourselves and be productive all the time. A lot of the time, we lack confidence in our abilities because we don't try to challenge ourselves. For example, there have been times when I have lacked confidence in public speaking but at the same time, I still don't have much experience in doing it. I have spoken in front of audiences before and it has been a nerve-wracking experience that left me in a bit of a sweat. But the fear of public speaking is a common fear, and maybe that's what was in my mind. People can become apt public speakers, with practice. So, I now take a different approach... I don't avoid the opportunities to speak in public, I embrace the chance to step out of my comfort zone and confront my fear head on!

The key is to not let your body language undermine what it is you want to communicate. Since a large part of communication comes from body language, which includes posture and facial expressions, by taking care in the messages you put out, you become more aware of the image you're projecting, and this (believe it or not) will build a more confident you.

TASKS - Take some confidence boosting action!

Here are a number of tasks you can carry out, all of them designed to help boost your confidence.

Make a Vision Board
Making a vision board is something I have enjoyed doing on many occasions. I have done this for business numerous times and it has created some very powerful results (I even created vision board backgrounds for my phone so that every time I looked at my phone, I would see what I wanted to implement or bring into my life).

Vision boards work. I believe if you see it, it becomes more real. If you believe it, you can achieve it. But first you must see it!

If you write something down, you are more likely to achieve it. In seeing it (and seeing it every day), it becomes more and more real. Many times, we see vision board examples that seem somewhat materialistic (big house, expensive car …) and this is fine, but for this task, I would like you to think on another level. When you make a vision board, you are putting out a message to the universe and telling it what you want.

First things first, you need to truly understand the meaning and purpose behind your vision board, and cultivate a positive mindset. The vision board is not magic on its own, but with the correct mindset, and ambition, the results can be magical. So choose the pictures and words for the vision board intentionally, and understand that you have to put in work in order for the vision board to work.

Getting prepared...

Some of you might be able to do the preparation for creating a vision board in your mind – it might simply be a question of finding a quiet space, allowing yourself to relax and allow the thoughts to enter your mind. For others, you might prefer to make notes first. If so, use **The Positivity Journal** to jot down your thoughts as they occur to you.

Start by reflecting on the current year. Why? Because it's a good idea to build upon your accomplishments from the current year when you're thinking about / writing goals for the upcoming year. It helps you to create measurable goals, and continue to grow in specific areas of your life.

Think about which areas of your life you want to improve or grow in – spiritual, emotional, intellectual, social, physical, environmental, occupational, and financial. Develop goals for each life area and reflect on the steps you need to take in order to reach those goals. This process helps to ensure that you pay attention to all areas of your life as opposed to only focusing on the one that may stand out to you the most in the moment. This is important because all these life areas work together and contribute to your overall wellness and satisfaction. If one area is particularly suffering, it can negatively affect other areas of your life and your overall balance.

Think about the bucket list stuff too! That might include places you want to travel to, new things you want to experience, fun things you want to do, new food you want to try, anything that comes to mind! Your list should include things that add some spice and excitement to your life, and switch things up from your regular routine.

Set the mood – it's really important to create a peaceful space, and cultivate a positive mindset before putting your vision board together. You don't want any negative vibes to interfere with your process because you're going to need all the positive vibes you can get! The vision board is all about manifesting positive energy into your life, so start this project off on the right foot. Create a calm environment for yourself and make sure you have enough space to be creative. You could light some candles, diffuse some essential oils, play calming music, meditate … do whatever it takes to get you feeling relaxed, motivated, and inspired.

Materials needed:
- Large sheet of paper / poster board / cork board
- Scissors
- Glue
- Selection of magazines, brochures etc that you don't mind cutting up

Flick through the magazines and cut out the images and/or words that appeal to you, and that you think represent your goals, hopes and dreams. After you've found all your images it's time to let the creative vibes flow. This is pretty self explanatory, and there's really no right or wrong way to do this. Stick your images on your vision board whichever way looks right to you! You can add words to it – ones cut out from magazines or written on by hand; make it something that you'll be happy to see every day. Something that truly represents you and your dream life.

Hang your vision board up somewhere where you'll see it often, most likely your bedroom, office, or any other room where you spend a lot of time.

Look at your vision board every day to remind yourself of what you're working towards, and to help you stay focused.

Visualise your dream life when you look at your vision board as vividly as possible. Think positive thoughts, and think about what you need to do to make that life a reality.

Look to your vision board when you're feeling discouraged, lost, stuck, confused, frustrated, etc. Pull inspiration and motivation from your vision board when you're feeling these negative emotions. Because you created your vision board while you were feeling happy & inspired, looking at your vision board will evoke those positive emotions in you!

When you start to visualise achieving your dreams in this way, you will start to feel great, and notice how much it boosts your confidence.

You can do this activity with someone else too, for example make a shared vision board with your child / children. It's a lovely way to develop your relationships with others. Children are great at manifestation because they use their imagination a lot. So making a vision board with a child can really help bring all your visions to life.

Practise Mindfulness
Mindfulness is an approach that is about paying attention, on purpose, in a non-judgemental way. It's a practice that is scientifically proven to calm down your mind and slow down habitual thinking patterns, those that often lead to insecure, negative thoughts or contribute to a lack of confidence and low self-esteem.

We are constantly focusing on 'what's next' or what happened in the past, which leads to little awareness about what we need in the now. Adding in small doses of mindfulness is an incredibly powerful way to get us in a calmer state of mind. It's a way of paying attention to whatever is happening in our lives, which brings us more control. When we slow down, we make better decisions and feel more confident in our choices.

Now this doesn't mean you have to hit the yoga mat for long periods of time. Rather, mindfulness can be a quick tool that brings us into the here and now. It allows us to recognise the moment; it will not eliminate all of life's pressures but, with practice, it can help us respond to them in a calmer manner that benefits our mind and body.

Follow these steps to start on your mindfulness journey:
- Notice the present experience – focus on the sight, smell, taste, hear, feel
- Allow yourself to focus on your breathing and/or the experience fully
- Allow thoughts to come up, avoid judging them, just refocus as you can
- Attempt to allow yourself to fully engage in the experience
- Stay focused on the moment and the experience
- Try to let go of any negative thoughts about yourself or the experience

The following ten mindfulness techniques can easily be incorporated into your day. You'll soon see improved self-confidence and self-trust.

Walking with the senses: notice where you are – the temperature, the scents, what is around you, what is unique about the situation, the colours, the people, and focus on what is happening in the moment.

On your way to work, listen to music and try to focus on one instrument or voice for the entire song. Notice how this changes your experience.

Try a guided mediation; you can search YouTube for quick guided meditations. This helps you get in touch with your body. Do these during break at work or any time you need to get centered.

Eat with your senses. In our busy world, we tend to rush everything, inhaling food at our desk or in front of the TV. Instead, pay attention to each bite, the texture, tastes and feelings that come up. You are likely to enjoy it more and even eat less.

In your head, play a game, think of every food item that starts with the letter H, or all the cities that end in E. Focus on this for a few minutes and see if the thoughts you had before are as strong.

Try making up a short story in your mind. Think of it as a child's story – one you may read to an 8-year-old, for example. When you make up your next story, you could take on one of the roles in the story, taking yourself on a short journey to one of your own goals. Play around with the way you tell the story – who knows where it will take you?

Flowing thoughts: allow thoughts to come and go. This is a personal favourite. Find a quiet place (I do this when I am early for the school pick up, and am sitting waiting in my car) and close your eyes. See what thoughts and images come into your head. Let them come and go. It's really interesting to observe the kinds of thoughts and images that pop up – they usually have great relevance.

Empty your mind. Try this for a minute at a time at first, then increase the length of time each time you have a go. Try and keep a completely empty mind for one minute. Every time something shows up, go back to the emptiness. This can be hard at first but with practice, it becomes easier. Practice makes progress. Give it a whirl. Think of it as 'brain rest'. It's particularly beneficial to anyone with a very busy and active mind.

Balance the mind. Imagine a pair of scales in your mind. Imagine that this pair of scales represents your mind. One side logic; one side intuition. Visualise the scales in your mind as perfectly balanced. Both your mind and your emotions must be well-balanced and functioning optimally for you to achieve the happiness, health, and success you really want. By planting this balanced image in your mind, and returning to it when you need to, you can stay focused on what you want to create and make of yourself.

Feed your mind – give it positive brain food. Close your eyes and imagine the top of your head opening up, and then imagine a jug (or similar item of your choice) pouring positive words into your mind. See them falling into your mind. Close your mind and feel these words being absorbed, just as our food is absorbed into our bodies. In your mind's eye, see these words flowing around your body and being absorbed into your blood stream. Select words that are relevant to you. For example, if you feel low on energy, perhaps you will pour words such as energy, vibrance, vigour, fizz, sparkle, shine, excitement and so on, into your mind.

Mindfulness is a practice in loving yourself. Allow yourself to settle into whatever arises for you in this process. When your mind wanders 'off track' and you don't stick to something, that is perfectly fine. As soon as you notice that you've wandered from the path, you are present and can invite yourself to start it up again. It really is a process, and much like the way someone catches the words coming out of their mouth and thinks about them before speaking, mindfulness follows a similar pattern. You work to catch your mind from wandering off, and you bring it back on track. This takes time, so be kind to yourself and enjoy the process.

Create a confidence bubble

Surrounding yourself in a 'bubble' of confidence is a great help in guiding you through difficult situations – quite literally, step inside it when you need to tame those inner voices trying to knock you down, telling you you're not good enough, not smart enough, not fit enough...

It's a technique that can be done anywhere. I also do this for protection. I create a bubble of protection. It helps protect my energy, staves off negative thoughts and makes me feel safe.

First, work out why you need your bubble – what is bothering you right now? Is there something bringing you down, holding you back, or causing anxiety?

Now bring your bubble to life – what does it look, feel, and sound like? Be creative here! I often use a white light to surround me, with another layer of fire, then some spears facing outwards – giving me three layers of protection. In your bubble, you can have words / sounds / people / images and so on with you. I often picture Archangel Michael standing with a drawn sword just outside of my bubble, warding off any negative emotions / people / situations, for example.

Now the fun part. Start blowing up your bubble – blow in the colours, sounds, and image, and make it as big as you want – bring it to life. You can either blow up the bubble around you, or you can create it first and then step inside it.

Once inside your bubble, observe your surrounding, notice how you feel now that you are inside the bubble.

Step outside again, but take all the feelings with you; notice how you feel now. Are you still as bothered or worried about the thing you were stressing over before you stepped into the bubble?

Bring bubble back whenever you need it. Repeat the exercise from the beginning each time, as this will strengthen your bubble.

The exercise serves not just to let go of negative thoughts and emotions but to help you relax, focus, and harness creativity.

When a negative thought enters your mind, think three positive ones. Train yourself to flip the script.

One-minute confidence booster
If you don't have a lot of time to spare, here's a really quick but effective confidence booster:

Send yourself a positive daily text message (each day, say something different). Say something positive to you each and every day. You can write this using "I am..." or "You are..." It can be as simple as "I am happy" to something lengthier such as "You are going to have a fantastic day today. You are going to ace that job interview and you are going to smile your way through the day." Open the message as if someone has sent it to you and read it. Then smile.

7

Confidence and Appearance

Let's start by talking a little about self-acceptance. Self-acceptance is the cornerstone for living with more confidence. It enables you to recognise your strengths and weaknesses. It allows you to walk with a loving awareness of your humanity, the good parts and the flaws. Self-acceptance enables you to embody your strengths to lead a life that is in alignment with your core beliefs, values, and priorities.

Accepting yourself as you are right now will help you to recognise that you don't have to be a carbon copy of someone else to live a confident and successful lifestyle. Self-acceptance doesn't happen when you hate the person you are. It happens when you love yourself enough to believe that you are enough. It happens when you raise your personal standards knowing that you can do better and that you deserve better. Loving and accepting yourself is your natural state. Being critical and harsh towards yourself is a learned behaviour that you have the power to transform.

Do bear in mind that self-acceptance doesn't miraculously happen overnight. It takes extensive work and considerable dedication. But learning how to love yourself right and treat yourself well can impact the way you live your life and the things you're able to accomplish.

"Know your honour and your worth."

Here are some ways to jumpstart your journey to self-acceptance and take conscious action to make your life much fuller and more magical:

Be kind to yourself
No one judges you more than you judge yourself. You can be your own worst enemy, so you need to get out of your way, and start developing patience. Be patient with yourself, and accept your flaws as a positive source of personal growth and learning.

Confront your fears
We all have history that includes some bad, painful, or devastating experiences. We all have a past; we're human, and we're bound to be hurt by something. But it's the fear of the unknown that keeps us trapped.   When we are afraid to experience the new because it's unfamiliar, we allow ourselves to become stuck. It's important to take baby steps to create change. Don't become stuck in the mud. Start by making a list of the things that scare you. Start with one small thing (eg, not going to an exercise class because everyone who goes to it looks stronger and fitter than you), try to face it, and understand why it's not so scary. Then move onto the next small thing, and so on. Often the thought of doing something is much scarier than actually doing it. Go for it!

Stay positive
Surround yourself with goodness. Write yourself kind notes. Hang up posters with positive affirmations. Download an app on your phone that will send you inspirational quotes on a daily basis. When you feel insecurity and doubt creeping into your thoughts, turn to one of your positive 'go-tos'. Tell that little defeating voice inside your head to be quiet and that you refuse to listen to it.

Accept imperfection

Let go of what you think is 'the ideal'. Let go of what you think perfection looks like. Life is perfection in all its imperfections. Don't let a need for perfection slow you down in accomplishing your goals. Good is good enough. Perfection isn't real. And if you are looking for or waiting for perfection, you are always shifting the goal posts. You will continue to live your life chasing perfection. What is perfect to you? What does it look like / feel like? Moments can be perfect, but life on the whole cannot. Perfection is imperfection.

Don't take it personally

If something offends you, stop and ask yourself why you're offended. Make a conscious effort to stop assuming you know what people mean. Chances are people don't want to hurt you to begin with, but they might not know how to communicate effectively either. Things get lost in translation. If you're not clear on the meaning of a specific comment, all you have to do is ask. It has been said that if something is said to you and it offends you, then it's actually you that has the problem... Food for thought...

Forgive

You can't grow without forgiveness. Forgive others for things they didn't mean to do. Forgive others for things they didn't know they did. Forgive yourself for mistakes you think you've made. And forgive yourself if things don't change quickly enough, or work out as you had hoped. Forgive them for they know not what they do! Forgive you, for you know not what you do!

Believe in yourself
You are capable of accomplishing great things. Believe that you can do anything because you can. You are a strong and powerful being, and you can deal with any challenge that comes your way. Remember, you've already survived the worst thing you've experienced in your life. I truly believe that we would never be dealt any hands that we are not capable of coping with, and that actually what we are dealt will work lessons for us and allow us to grow. Believe that you can!

Don't give up – no matter what!
When you fall, you need to get up and keep going. Regardless. It's in our failures, not our successes, that we learn the most about ourselves. Figure out what motivates you by celebrating something you find challenging, or even failed at. It's in these intimate moments that life's precious lessons are learned. Reflect on this and see what lessons you learned. Maybe you could write these down in **The Positivity Journal**.

I failed at…
This made me feel…
This helped me learn…

"You yourself, as much as anybody in the entire universe, deserve your love & affection."
Buddha

8

Confidence and the influence of social media

Humans possess a fundamental drive to compare themselves with others. This serves many different functions such as evaluating the self, making decisions, being inspired and regulating emotions and wellbeing.

Social comparison can be beneficial when it inspires people to become more like the person they look up to, but it often causes people to feel inadequate, have poorer self-esteem and negative feelings.

Social networking sites provide the perfect platform for 'perfect' self-presentation by allowing users to select content on their profiles, post pictures, and represent themselves in 'ideal' ways that are far removed from reality.

Recent studies have found that frequent social media users believe that other users are happier and more successful, especially when they do not know them very well offline. So people are comparing their realistic offline selves to the idealised online selves of others, and that's obviously going to be detrimental to wellbeing.

We're all human. There are only so many celebrations of people's seemingly perfect lives that you can take until you start to criticise yourself and/or question your own worthiness. We instinctively engage in 'social comparison', which is where you start to look at others to see how you stack up.

Social comparison never ends well and can diminish your self-esteem because, as they say, you end up comparing your own behind-the-scenes with someone else's highlight reel. I know I have done it myself! In fact, it was one of the reasons I turned off my social media for a long period of time. I felt like it was a competition and when I actually stopped to consider my own core beliefs, I realised I believed that the only competition should be yourself; become the best version of you!

I highly recommend minimising social media usage, especially at times when you're feeling off. You might even consider installing a tool that automatically blocks your social media newsfeeds, so you can't give in to temptation. Take a week off social media and see how it affects you.

Any time I have taken a break from social media, I have felt renewed! It has enabled me to return to it with a completely different view on it. After one such break, I was inspired to create a positivity and confidence social media page, where I post inspirational and motivational quotes, and am connected with like-minded people. It's a joy to go on this page; I feel humbled by what I read and see.

When all is said and done, it's incredibly hard to get a real, genuine energy from social media pages.

Consider how social media can best serve you and stick with it. If you find it's making you feel inadequate, if it's having a negative impact on how you feel about yourself, it's time to move away from it, or at least re-think how it can fit into your life without impairing your self-esteem.

When I came off my social media for the best part of the year, I made the most of the time it freed up ... and wrote this book!

Task - Social Media Detox
For this task, all you will need is **The Positivity Journal**, (or a notebook) and a strong will!

Starting a detox is easy. The hard part is sticking with it. And while a detox doesn't have to be forever, you may decide after a few months that a permanent leave from social media is the best thing for you – and that's okay.

STEP 1: Designate technology-free times
We all experience times when we feel overexposured to social media, and perhaps to the internet in general, so designate time to completely unplug. Maybe for a few hours before bed each night, or perhaps better still, during the morning. Remember, what you see will be absorbed for the day ahead, so find a time that works for you. And when you do step away from the screens, make note of how you feel during that time, and afterwards. Are you less stressed? You can keep track of your feelings in **The Positivity Journal** or a notebook.

A study carried out in America found that students who unplugged from all technology for just one day experienced greater focus and better quality of life. Obviously unplugging isn't a cure-all for happiness, though. The key is to replace time spent on social media and technology with other beneficial things. Try replacing social media time with listening to positivity affirmations on YouTube! Time well spent – I guarantee you that! Better still, if you spend that digital-free time focusing on your relationships and activities you enjoy, you can really make your life better.

STEP 2: Set social media time limits for yourself
Along the same lines as technology-free times, try setting time limits on your personal social media use.

But before you embark on setting limits for yourself, make sure your goal is realistic. Over the course of a typical weekday, keep a written record in **The Positivity Journal** of every time you check social media, and if it's for work or personal reasons. You may be using it a lot more than you think, so make sure your time limits are feasible for you to achieve.

STEP 3: Prioritise other activities, hobbies, and passions
Have a think – what activities or hobbies would you have more time for if you re-dedicated the time you spend social networking?

Instead of framing it as a social media break, you're more likely to stick to the detox if you're working toward something you want, as opposed to taking something away. Try reading those books that have been piling up (unread), learning a new language, or sticking to a gym routine to replace the time you'd normally spend on social media to make your detox extra productive. This can help you prolong the detox and better still turn the detox into a new way of living for yourself. Hooray!

STEP 4: Turn off mobile notifications
A simple way to discourage checking your feeds over and over might be turning off mobile notifications. If you aren't constantly notified about what's going on online, you might be less inclined to check it on your phone so often. Navigate to your phone's settings and choose how you hear from social media apps on your phone to take a break (indirectly, at least).

Make sure you make a regular note in **The Positivity Journal** of how your detox makes you feel, ideally at the end of each day and each week (if you are going for a longer digital-free stretch).

Regain control of the way you spend your time – and how you feel about yourself. Feed your mind, body and soul the old fashioned way!

9

Confidence and the subconscious mind

Something I have learned – the guidance of the subconscious mind that produces your dreams can also help you build your self-confidence and develop your intelligence. By tapping into it, I have been able to stop making mistakes and learn how to always do what will help me succeed in life. Sounds crazy, maybe? It's true though. Let me explain...

My self-confidence is based on the transformation of my personality. My life has been a rollercoaster journey, no two ways about it! There have been times I have hit rock bottom and I have had to work very hard on myself to get back to a place of content. I have had to build myself back up each time and work to maintain my confidence, and try to catch it when I can feel it falling. Something I have learned to do now is to be very mindful of my words and actions – not something I always did in the past! I control my behaviour and always act after pondering all the alternatives I have at my disposal in all circumstances. This means that I am able to keep my confidence rolling happily along. It has taken patience and development of mindfulness and awareness over the years. I now feel powerful (and stronger and wiser) for it.

Having nurtured a more peripheral vision, I have more trust in my own capacities. I am able, to a certain extent, to predict the future and detect dangers, mistakes, and other negative factors that can generate potential problems. I am able to prepare for the positive future results I desire. I feel safe, I have the courage to face the adversities of life. That's because I truly believe that I can tackle the problems that come my way, surpass obstacles, and triumph in the end.

Why do I believe this? I believe this because I trust my subconscious. I believe that inner power will build your self-confidence. However, in order to believe in your inner power, you have to eliminate wrong concepts and behavioral abnormalities, which prevent you from feeling strong.

You can learn more about your subconscious mind via my **Confidence Cards**. (See page 81 onwards).

10

Food and confidence

What does food have to do with confidence, you might ask. A whole lot, it turns out!

I'm sure we've all eaten more chocolate than we intended to, reached for a few more biscuits … only to feel a bit peeved with ourselves later. If you are eating an unbalanced diet and have erratic meal patterns, it's likely that you feel demotivated and less confident. That's certainly true in my case. I have been through periods of letting my diet slip (too much fast food while on the go), and my levels of confidence go right down with it. When I am eating healthily, I feel better about myself and this naturally spills over into other areas of my life.

I consider myself a healthy, physically fit woman and I am grateful for the body and lifestyle I have been given and work with. However, I do have a pretty fast-paced routine, and there are times when I find myself making poor diet choices, which in turn leaves me feeling in a bit of a slump, both physically and mentally. I took it upon myself to change that, living by the motto: If I can change it; I will!

Over the years, I have tried a number of ways to get myself back to my normal energetic and creative ways, only to find myself falling back into my bad habits a few weeks later. I once attended an incredibly powerful nutrition workshop where the nutritionist said these words:

"We are so used to feeling like crap, we don't know how good we should be feeling".

And boy, was she right! When I was introduced to Ayurveda, things became very, very different.

Ayurveda is a form of complementary and alternative medicine that dates back to about 5000 years. In Ayurveda, your individual nature is mirrored in your body type, known as 'dosha'. The doshas reflect 3 main governing principles of nature – Vata (air), Pitta (fire), and Kapha (earth-water). Each person is a unique combination of these doshas, with different proportions of each existing within. I am a 50-50 combination of Pitta and Vata.

Your dosha depicts what and how you eat, how you exercise, when you sleep, and even where you prefer to live.

There are different Ayurvedic protocols and recommendations for the 3 different body types, including herbs, diet, exercise, lifestyle, skin, and digestion.

Being aware of your dosha allows you to identify Ayurvedic protocols to align your internal nature with the larger cycles of nature, such as the daily rhythms and seasonal cycles. It's like having a map that leads you closer to your best self, so that you can reach your true potential, and be more radiant and joyful.

And it works! I speak from experience. When I started following an Ayurvedic lifestyle, for the first time in my life, I felt fully alive! I slept like a log, I lost weight, my anxiety dissipated and my energy levels soared to new heights!

When you begin practising an Ayurvedic lifestyle, what you are really doing is starting a journey of self-discovery, mindfulness, and awareness. With this, comes an improvement in your overall wellbeing and your spiritual growth.

By adapting my habits to my dosha type, I gained vitality and wellbeing. I started getting to know my dosha with food: I began to listen to my body on a daily basis and adjusted the flavours of food depending on how I was feeling. At first, this seemed difficult, but once I began to understand how the flavours influence mind and body, it became fun, and opened up creative ways of eating and cooking.

When I embarked on my Ayurveda journey, a typical day looked like this:

6am: Rise and practise a morning meditation (I interchanged this with positive affirmations audios)

Detox hot drink – lime, apple cider vinegar, cold pressed honey (added when drink cools)

Yoga sequences – I was particularly attracted to nurturing flow sequences, but practised a range of styles, depending on my energy levels and time available to practise.

Self massage with sesame oil – This is actually about self love, about treating your body with love and care. Pure TLC. The oil is rich in minerals and antioxidants, which are easily absorbed into the skin. My skin felt so soft.

Breakfast: stewed apples, pears and prunes

I found that I was very hungry at first, so I kept busy, which helped me avoid snacking. I also had my lunch around 11:30 and this was my biggest meal of the day.

Lunch: Ayurveda recipes designed around my Vata / Pitta dosha. The balance that suits me best is 60% vegetables, 20% carbs, 20% protein. I aim to consume at least 3 different types of vegetables (with limited intake of potatoes). This should be the biggest meal of the day. At this stage, I still ate white meat and fish (I have since turned vegan), so lunch usually consisted of a slice of salmon with carrots, mange tout, broccoli and brown rice. Often, there were specific Vata / Pitta detoxifying recipes such as Agni soup or Kitchari.

With my meals all planned and prepared, I got busy living and kept my mind active and focused. It is easy to slip into thinking about food and craving specific foods, especially when you know you cannot have them. I avoided supermarkets. I did online shopping so that I didn't have to face all the sugar on sale at supermarkets. I also worked on my lower chakras (via guided meditations) as I knew this would help empower me and my determination, enhancing personal power and self discipline, which were so very important while following the Ayurveda programme.

Dinner: Ayurveda recipes designed for my dosha, typically fresh soups, and not much else! If I felt hungry, I would have a few more vegetables on the side.

I also had digestive herbs and Triphala to take before and after meal times. Triphala is an Ayurvedic herbal formulation consisting of three fruits native to the Indian subcontinent: Amalaki, Bibhitaki, and Haritaki. The combination of the three fruits has a synergistic effect to bolster many systems in the body, including the GI tract, respiratory, urinary, cardiovascular and nervous systems. For all its incredible properties, there's no getting away from its awful taste! I had to down it in one. However, the Triphala combined with the herbs worked to improve my digestive system and support regular bowel movements. I had no bloating whatsoever, and I believe it was down to these formulations.

The definite no-gos of the programme were:

Caffeine
Alcohol
Refined sugars (limited intake of fruit for natural sugar)
Dairy products
Red meat
Wheat

It was also important not to overeat; I had to stop eating before I felt full to allow space in my stomach for efficient digestion. My coach told me that meal sizes should be no bigger than what you could cup in your own two hands held out together side-by-side! Yikes!

I had to leave a minimum of 4-6 hours between meals to ensure the stomach was empty. There was strictly no eating after 7pm, and no drinks 30 minutes before and after meals. Oh, and no snacking! This was incredibly difficult, even with my strong will and iron determination! I had to keep my mind strong. I'm the type of person who is 'all in' when I commit to something. That doesn't mean, however, that it was an easy ride; in fact, it was one of the hardest things I've ever had to do. I had to practise huge self-discipline, and I felt proud of myself for acknowledging its importance, and doing something to strengthen it. Life puts challenges and problems on the path to success and achievement, and in order to rise above them, we have to act with perseverance and persistence, and this of course, requires self-discipline. Working on this skill leads to better self-confidence and self esteem, and consequently, to greater happiness and satisfaction.

They say if you can control what you eat and drink then you can control anything in your life!

To stick to any kind of detox, I would advise the following:

Be prepared – planning ahead is key! I prepared all my meals in the morning and if I was on the go, I took my food with me. I basically put food first and worked out the rest of my life from there!

Where possible, work around your detox. I planned any meetings after lunch and I avoided working late which meant I would eat late.

Avoid social situations where you may be tempted by food and drink that is not part of the detox. While this may not always be possible, try to clear your diary in the early stages of the detox while you are still building resilience!

Keep your mind strong, and don't be influenced or steered off course by others. It's so easy to meet with friends and grab a quick bite to eat – one fast food meal won't hurt, right? That one meal leads to the next one and the next one and before you know it, you're back in the bad habits cycle.

Always keep your 'why' in the forefront of your mind. Why are you doing this? When you bring your mind back to this question, it will be easier to resist urges.

If you start to feel as though you might cave, move quickly. Go for a walk – get away from the fridge!

Don't listen to the opinions of others. People often like to tell you how you should live your life, particularly your family. You do you. Do what you want and live the way you want. Say no to people if you need to, and stay true to your goals.

Don't let circumstances or situations affect the detox and/or your journey. Stay on your pathway regardless of what may pop up during that time, whether it's a date or an impromptu celebration. Say no thank you to the wine and chocolates. Drink water – it's okay!

Work on your lower chakras via meditation, as this will help build your self-discipline.

Make new connections – friendship is a two-way street, and the 'give' side of the give-and-take contributes to your own sense of self-worth, elevating your mood, and reducing the urge to reach for comfort foods. Being there for others makes you feel valued and adds a greater purpose to your life.

Understand yourself – ask yourself why you are feeling pulled towards eating chocolate? Is it because you are lacking in some area of your life? Perhaps replacing chocolate with self-love will help reduce the amount of chocolate you crave.

Hold onto the feelings of feeling better – that day you ate so well, slept so soundly, went to the gym – how that made you feel. That's what you want. More days like that.

Be prepared to feel not so great to begin with. Any detox always has a big kick to it. Everyone feels it differently. Headachy, lethargic, fuzzy-headed and so on. Stick with it – it will pass!

So what were the effects of this routine on me? Well, it was a tough first few days. It was one of the most self-disciplined experiences I have ever undertaken. A lot of the time, I just wanted to eat cake. I craved sugar and I had bad headaches in the beginning, but by day 4, I was sleeping better than I had done in months, or years maybe. By day 6, I felt as though I had been reborn! By day 10, I had lost half a stone. My body felt light, my mind was calm and collected, and I felt so alive!

Through incorporating a diet specifically tailored to my body, its energy and its needs, I found clarity. It had a positive effect on my mindfulness, and my stress levels were significantly reduced.

The idea that food can affect our mood and behaviour isn't new and researchers have found some fascinating links between what we eat and mental health. When it comes to confidence and self-esteem, considering your diet and making any necessary changes can help to reduce anxiety, boost your mood and in turn help you feel better about yourself and more confident.

It's all about getting the right balance of nutrients from foods, which can help our mood and the way we feel. For example, eating carbohydrate-rich foods make the brain receive more serotonin – a hormone that makes you feel positive, relaxed and confident. Too many foods or drinks that are high in sugar or caffeine, however, can cause mood fluctuations, which can leave you feeling lethargic, irritable and anxious. Some research also suggests that low levels of vitamins, minerals and essential fatty acids can affect our mental health; for example, links have been seen between depression and low levels of omega-3 oils. I truly believe you are what you eat!

For those that like structure, Ayurveda is easy to follow and leaves little room to deviate. It may be an adjustment at first, but think of it as eating the foods you were always meant to eat. If you are looking to bring lasting change into your diet, health or even your life, Ayurveda might be just the thing! With strong guidelines that have been proven for centuries, consider it an all-encompassing wellness plan designed to bring true transformation to every aspect of your life.

The final hour...

I really hope this book has helped you begin or keep on your journey to self-belief, and I hope you continue to use the book within your life whenever you see fit.

May you feel empowered to help yourself as you go on your journey of self -discovery.

These lyrics from Bob Marley's incredibly influential Redemption Song have the power to inspire and liberate us all ...

"Emancipate yourselves from mental slavery;
None but ourselves can free our minds."
Bob Marley (Redemption Song)

I am truly grateful to you for being a part of my journey. I appreciate you.

Yours truly,
Amy Elizabeth x

With you every step of the way...

Online self-help content - you can join my Patreon tribe and become part of the 'Beyond Ace' community allowing access to daily self-help content, delivered directly to you. Videos, tutorials, reading recommendations, daily boosts, affirmations, tools and techniques and much more, right at your fingertips. Join me there and read more at:
www.patreon.com/AmyElizabeth

Holistic healing - accessing holistic healing was fundamental to my personal journey. Reiki, Crystal Healing, Hopi Ear Candles and The Bars - Access Consciousness can all be booked via email:
goodvibes@amyelizabeth.org.uk

Healing bracelets and empowering accessories / jewellery - These are more than just pretty bracelets – my collection of semi-precious stone and crystal bracelets can be worn for empowerment, balance and enlightenment. Crystals are handpicked to influence your energy by focusing the mind and emotions in a positive way. Wearing a healing bracelet serves as a constant reminder of the areas of life that you are working to improve. Having faith in the ability of the bracelet to work its magic is key. Please visit:
www.etsy.com/uk/shop/FromTheHeartLtd

"Amy I got your 'Strong Soul' bracelet in a shop in Nottingham just after my Indian grandma passed. I remember it saying strength on it. I wanted to say thank you as it has given me strength over the past few years - even if it has just been for the benefit my own mental state when I wear it..."

- Aneesha

In addition to my healing bracelets, I offer a range of jewellery that has been designed to enhance feelings of positivity and confidence. My diamond 'Be Ace' stud earrings and mens tie tacks and cuff links are some of my favourites. My gold and silver power band bracelets and my 'Success' gold power tags are other favourites of mine. Bespoke designs, engagement, wedding rings and collections are also available upon request. Full website coming soon at:
www.amyelizabeth.org.uk

Empowering clothing line
Fashion is an incredibly powerful tool when it comes to feeling confident. My collection of casual and urban clothing will make you look and feel great. With empowering slogans and bright colours, the collection is designed to boost the spirit. Remember, if a piece of clothing works for you and makes you feel good, then make it your signature look and rock it! Full website coming soon at:
www.amyelizabeth.org.uk

Pure, safe and beneficial products for health and wellness
Products to help you glow from the inside out. Swiss skin, hair and nutritional care unparalleled in quality. Vegan, free from harmful chemicals and animal cruelty free. Skin care consultations can be arranged. See more at:
www.amyelizabeth.arbonne.com

Let's connect

Life is a beach and then you live! Why not live life happily and to its fullest? I hope that this book has helped you in some way, and given you some ideas to kick-start your journey to a more fulfilled life through feeling better about yourself.

I would love to hear about your journey. Feel free to share any part of it with me, whether it's the small actions you have implemented every day to improve your confidence and retrain your brain to learn positive new ways of thinking and believing, or the challenges you have set yourself to stretch beyond your comfort zone of confidence to prove to yourself what you are truly capable of achieving.

With every incremental step forward, your confidence will grow. Success fuels success, so please share your stories. I am looking forward to hearing from you.

Email: **goodvibes@amyelizabeth.org.uk**
Instagram: **fromtheheartltd**
LinkedIn: **Amy Elizabeth**

Full website coming soon:
www.amyelizabeth.org.uk

To book Amy as a motivational guest speaker please email:
goodvibes@amyelizabeth.org.uk

To purchase Amy's **Affirmation Cards, The Positivity Journal** and **The Positivity Pack** (including **The Confidence Cards**) please visit:
www.thepositivitypack.com

RECOMMENDED READING AND VIEWING

There are so many other ways and resources available to assist you on your continued journey to self-discovery; seeing you all the way through life. It has been an absolute pleasure to be part of your journey.

Here are just a few of the books that have stayed with me and left a particularly powerful impression:

The Essential Guide to Foods that Heal – Suzannah Olivier

The Secret Language of Your Body – Inna Segal

Light Is the New Black – Rebecca Campbell

May Cause Miracles – Gabrielle Bernstein

Right Riches For You – Dr Dain Heer and Gary M. Douglas

Being You, Changing The World – Dr Dain Heer

Ask and It Is Given – Esther Hicks and Jerry Hicks

The Art of Happiness – HH Dalai Lama & Howard C. Cutler

Your Best Year Yet! – Jinny S Ditzler

Mindfulness Pocketbook: Little Exercises for a Calmer Life – Gill Hasson

Emotional Intelligence Pocketbook: Little Exercises for an Intuitive Life – Gill Hasson

The Secret - Rhonda Byrne

Daily Meditations for Practicing The Course – Karen Casey

The Art of Being Brilliant – Andy Cope and Andy Whittaker

Madly in Love with ME – Christine Arylo

A few recommendations for younger readers and teens (they can be read by adults too, or and those of you who like to read books with your children):

The Power of Henry's Imagination (The Secret) – Skye Byrne

Lionheart - Richard Collingridge

Little Roo and the Big Wide World - Guido Van Genechten

Silly Billy - Anthony Browne

You Are Awesome: Find Your Confidence and Dare to be Brilliant at (Almost) Anything – Matthew Syed

The Secret to Teen Power – Paul Harrington

VIDEOS & FILM

'Wonder' – starring Julia Roberts. This film shows us to always choose kindness, stand up for yourself, never judge anyone and – most importantly – be you! *"You can't blend in when you were born to stand out."*

'The Pursuit Of Happyness' – starring Will Smith. This film has a lot to offer. It shows us how to face adverse conditions and teaches strength in never giving up. It shows positive mental attitudes in characters as well as persistence and determination, and not letting others stand in your way. *"You got a dream, you gotta protect it. People can't do something themselves - they wanna tell you that you can't do it. You want something? Go get it. Period."*

'The Secret' Rhonda Byrne based on the international best-selling book by Rhonda Byrne, starring numerous highly respected and knowledgeable people. The film teaches us to embrace truth, difference and seeing things differently. Is your mind open to all possibilities? *"You become what you think about most…You are the masterpiece of your own life."*

'Pay It Forward' – starring Kevin Spacey. When one student creates a plan for "paying forward" favours, he creates a ripple effect of human kindness. A story about a young boy attempting to make the world a better place.

'Magic Beyond Words: The JK Rowling Story' – starring Poppy Montgomery. This film shows us strength and persistence at its finest. In the face of adversity push forward always and keep striving for what you want.

'Walt Before Mickey' – a film about Walt Disney and his journey. It shows integrity, courage and never giving up. *"Dreams don't come true without a lot of failure."*

'The Terminal' – starring Tom Hanks. This is a film about patience, the gift of listening to others and cultivating resilience.

'Sliding Doors' – starring Gwyneth Paltrow, this is a film about the 'almosts' and 'what ifs' shown through two parallel universes. Life lessons via painful experiences can teach us a lot about ourselves. We cannot control the outcomes of life but we can control our actions and choices.

'The Blind Side' – starring Sandra Bullock. A film about being non-judgemental, trusting your own instincts and speaking your mind. Strong messages about determination and dedication. You can do anything you set your mind to do. A strong sense of understanding that your situation doesn't define you - YOU define your situation. *"Courage is a hard thing to figure…"*

'Forrest Gump' – starring Tom Hanks. What messages does this film deliver? Expect the unexpected, cherish true friendships, believe in love, put the past behind you, listen to your heart, try something new and treat everyone equally. *"Life is like a box of chocolates, you never know what you're gunna get"*.

'Good Will Hunting' – starring Matt Damon and Robin Williams. There are some strong life lessons in this film including that life is about experiences, taking risks and stepping out of your comfort zone. *"You can do anything you want. You are bound by nothing."*

'Patch Adams' – starring Robin Williams. A film about compassion, happiness, helping others, fearlessness, seeing what others ignore, and kindness. Based on a true story. *"You treat a person, I guarantee you, you'll win, no matter what the outcome"*.

'Bruce Almighty' – starring Jim Carey. As much as we seek to control our lives and our surroundings, we can't. And in trying, we can alienate those around us. A film about free will and how we can work to count our blessings rather than our problems. *"No matter how filthy something gets, you can always clean it right up."*

'Queen Of Katwe' - starring Madina Nalwanga. A film showing us how our situation and surroundings do not determine our future. Anything is possible. Anything you put your mind to. Miracles happen everyday. *"Sometimes the place you are used to is not the place you belong."*

'Cool Runnings' - starring Doug E. Doug. A film about a bobsled team with dreams of competing in the winter olympics. Team work makes the dream work. *"Rise and shine! It's butt-whippin' time!"*

'Coach Carter' - starring Samuel L Jackson. A film about respect, team work and that winning isn't everything. *"Our deepest fear is that we are powerful beyond measure... There is nothing enlightened about shrinking so that other people wont feel insecure around you."*

Jason Stephenson's YouTube channel

"I was immediately drawn to Jason's channel because of his soothing yet powerful voice. I felt a connection. He has some super powerful videos with great calming visuals. He covers topics from anxiety, PTSD, and insomnia to reclaiming your personal power, balancing your chakras and meeting your spiritual guides. There is something for everyone, both guided and music-led meditations. Meditation changed my life. Period. I definitely have Jason to thank for helping me on my personal journey."

See who you connect with and go find your tribe!

You are welcome to keep a look out for my own youtube channel coming soon.

On my channel, you will find a selection of guided mediations and powerful affirmations that I have created to allow you to become more in tune with your thoughts and the way you think about yourself in general.

Like, subscribe and leave your comments - I'd love to read them!

ACKNOWLEDGEMENTS

Thank you to…

My son … for your patience and belief in me. You are so kind and compassionate.

My dad … you have been so supportive over the years, and I know you will always have my back.

My cherished friend, Susannah Bartram … for being the wisdom I sought. You are inspirational and have a heart of gold.

My cousin and loyal friend Kyrie-Leonah. You are supportive through thick and thin and together we shine bright.

My longtime friend, Limahl Rendel Mills … for sharing an everlasting entrepreneurial journey with me. Your strength and persistence is inspirational to me.

"Amy is an incredibly motivated entrepreneur and businesswoman. I have seen her overcome adversity over the years and come out the other end prosperous. Her innovative approach to business is most definitely her strong suit, and her likability and spirit is gravitational."
Limahl Rendel Mills

Sally Wathen … you helped me find inner peace. You are an incredible spiritual leader with a pure heart and bright light.

Chrissy Cain … you helped me understand myself. Your guidance has been gratefully received over the years.

A special note...

A special thank you to my amazing editor, Emma Sasai. Her patience is something we could wish for. Her magic touch meant everything to me and this book. A huge thank you from the bottom of my heart for her magical ways. One in a million!

Final words from Amy Elizabeth...

It's been an absolute pleasure to write this book. I sit here very humbled with a sense of wholeness, knowing that I have helped you in some way. I wish you a successful and happy continued journey.

Cheers to the future!

Pure Confidence

Walk your own path of self-belief –
for the rest of your living days.

Amy Elizabeth

ISBN: 9781096178248
Imprint: Independently published

Printed in Great Britain
by Amazon

39301639R00056